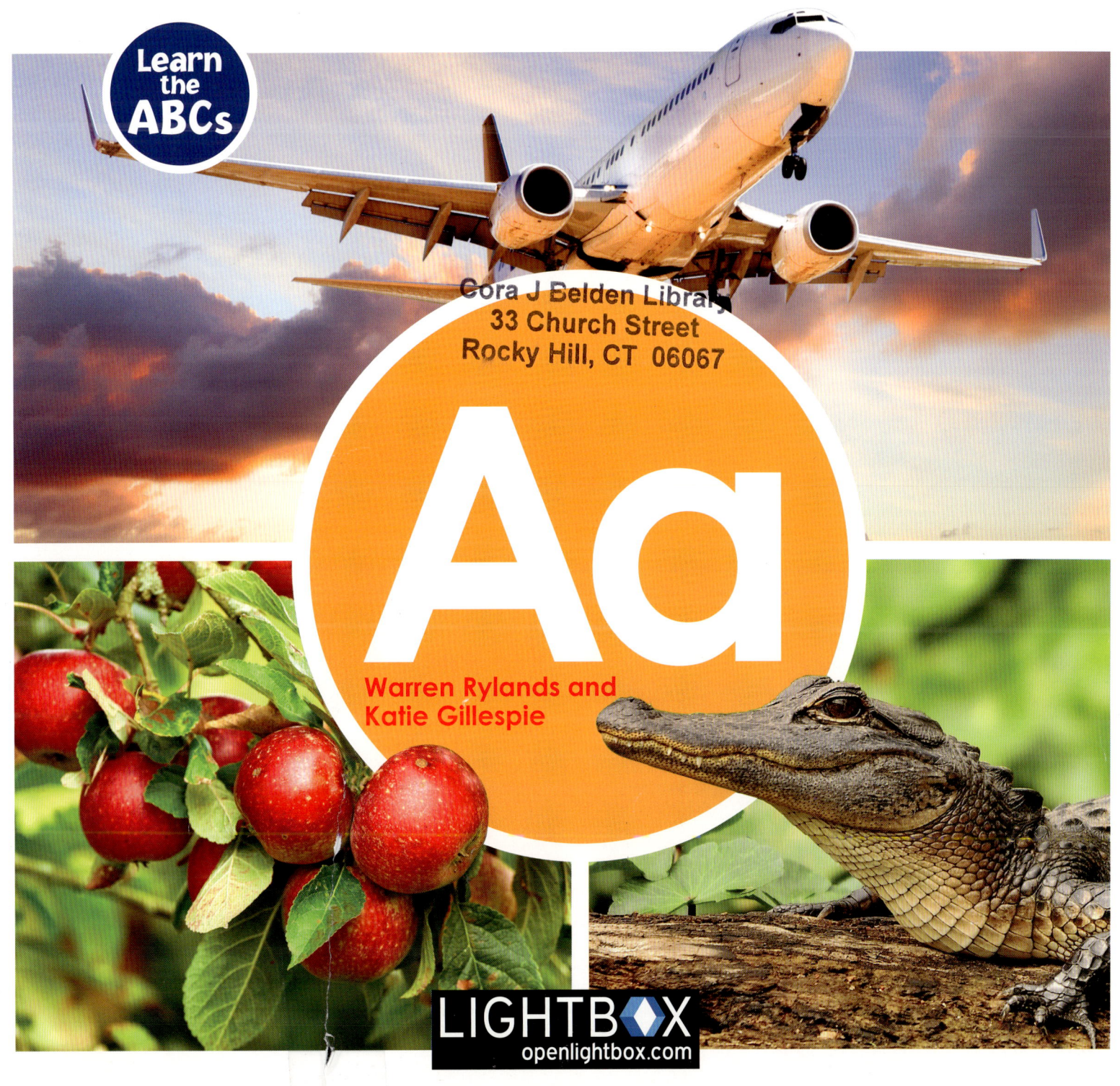

Learn the ABCs

Aa

Warren Rylands and
Katie Gillespie

LIGHTB◆X
openlightbox.com

LIGHTBOX

Go to
www.openlightbox.com
and enter this book's
unique code.

ACCESS CODE

L B X X 4 9 4 5

Lightbox is an all-inclusive digital solution for the teaching and learning of curriculum topics in an original, groundbreaking way. Lightbox is based on National Curriculum Standards.

OPTIMIZED FOR

✓ **TABLETS**
✓ **WHITEBOARDS**
✓ **COMPUTERS**
✓ **AND MUCH MORE!**

Copyright © 2022 Smartbook Media Inc. All rights reserved.

STANDARD FEATURES OF LIGHTBOX

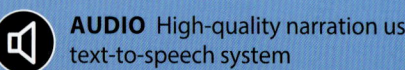
AUDIO High-quality narration using text-to-speech system

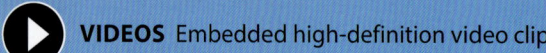
VIDEOS Embedded high-definition video clips

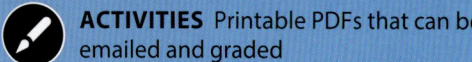
ACTIVITIES Printable PDFs that can be emailed and graded

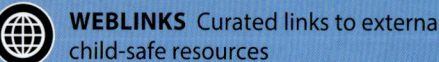
WEBLINKS Curated links to external, child-safe resources

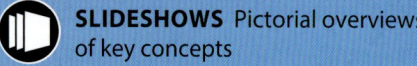
SLIDESHOWS Pictorial overviews of key concepts

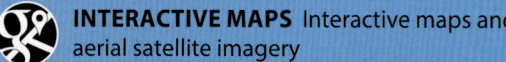
INTERACTIVE MAPS Interactive maps and aerial satellite imagery

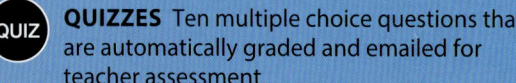
QUIZZES Ten multiple choice questions that are automatically graded and emailed for teacher assessment

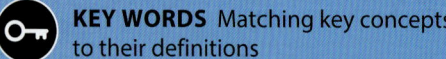
KEY WORDS Matching key concepts to their definitions

VIDEOS

WEBLINKS
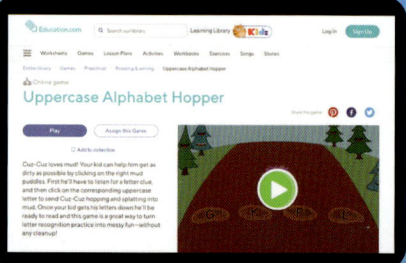

SLIDESHOWS

QUIZZES

This title is part of our Lightbox digital subscription

1-Year K–5 Subscription
ISBN 978-1-5105-5712-3

Access hundreds of Lightbox titles with our digital subscription.
Sign up for **a FREE** subscription trial at **www.openlightbox.com/trial**

Learn the ABCs

Aa

CONTENTS

3

Let's discover the letter

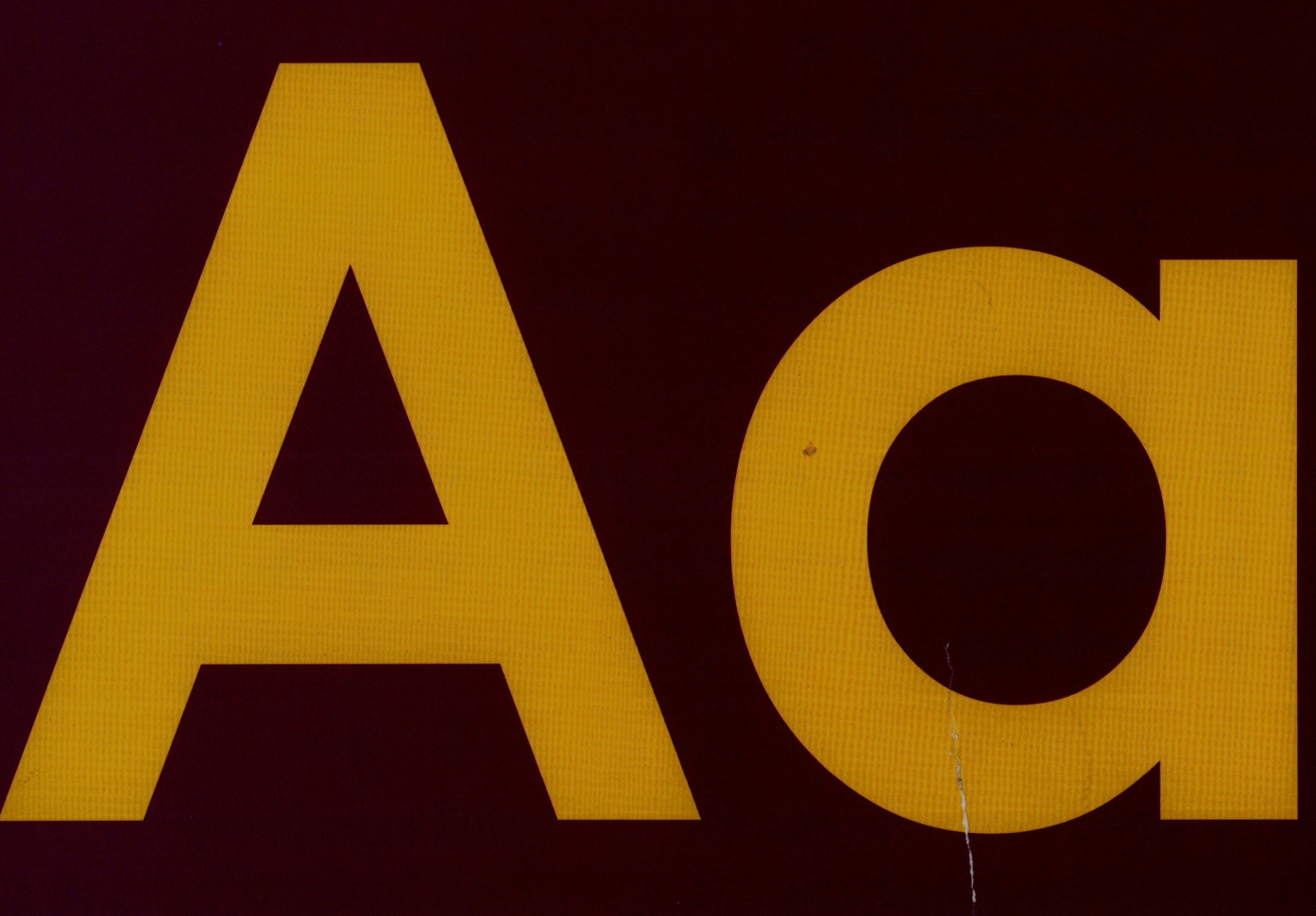

This is an uppercase A

This is how you write it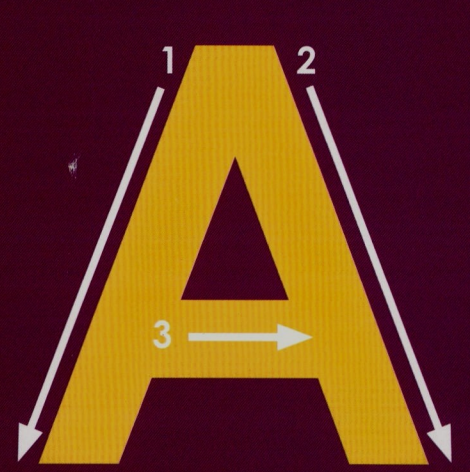

This is a lowercase a

This is how you write it

The letter **a** can start many words.

ants

alligators

airplane

apples

ape

The letter **a** can be inside a word.

cat

car

day

bat

ram

9

The letter **a** can be at the end of a word.

orca

pizza

sofa

banana

sea

Many names start with an uppercase **A**.

Alex is happy.

Aaron loves music.

Ana can jump high.

Amy likes to swim.

Anthony reads a story.

13

The letter a makes different sounds.

cake

hat

The word **cāke** has a long **ā** sound.

The word **hăt** has a short **ă** sound.

Some words have
a long **ā** sound.

fāce

dāy

chānge

lāter

cāme

Other words have
a short **ă** sound.

jăm

băck

ăbout

ănd

hăve

Having Fun with A

Andrew likes amazing animals.

There are always animals at the zoo.

Andrew and his family went to the zoo.

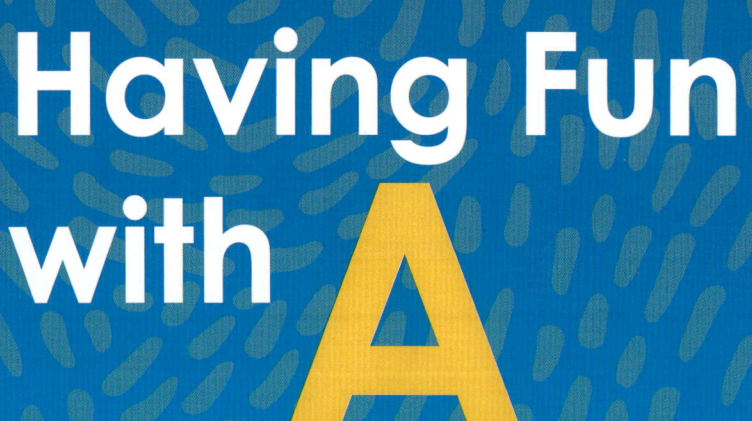

They saw all of the animals.
Alice the alligator was asleep.
Allan the ape was eating
an apple.
What an awesome adventure!

The alphabet has **26** letters.

A is the first letter in the alphabet.

Aa Bb Cc Dd

Ee Ff Gg Hh Ii Jj

Kk Ll Mm Nn Oo

Pp Qq Rr Ss Tt Uu

Vv Ww Xx Yy Zz

KEY WORDS

Research has shown that as much as 65 percent of all written material published in English is made up of 300 words. These 300 words cannot be taught using pictures or learned by sounding them out. They must be recognized by sight. This book contains 58 common sight words to help young readers improve their reading fluency and comprehension. This book also teaches young readers several important content words, such as proper nouns. These words are paired with pictures to aid in learning and improve understanding.

Page	Sight Words First Appearance
4	let, letter, the
5	a, an, how, is, it, this, write, you
6	can, many, start, words
8	be, car, day
10	at, end, of
11	sea
12	names, with
13	high, likes, reads, to, story
14	different, makes, sound
15	has, long
16	face, have, some
17	came, change, later
18	other
19	about, and, back
20	always, animals, are, family, his, there, went
21	all, saw, they, was, what
22	first, in

Page	Content Words First Appearance
4	Aa
6	ants, apples
7	airplane, alligators, ape
8	cat
9	bat, ram
10	orca, pizza
11	banana, sofa
12	Alex
13	Aaron, Amy, Ana, Anthony, music
14	cake, hat
18	jam
20	Andrew, fun, zoo
21	adventure, Alice, Allan
22	alphabet

Published by Smartbook Media Inc.
276 5th Avenue, Suite 704 #917
New York, NY 10001
Website: www.openlightbox.com

Library of Congress Cataloging-in-Publication Data

Names: Rylands, Warren, author. | Gillespie, Katie, author.
Title: Aa / Warren Rylands and Katie Gillespie.
Description: New York, NY : Smartbook Media Inc., [2022] | Series: Learn the ABCs | Audience: Grades K-1
Identifiers: LCCN 2020054160 (print) | LCCN 2020054161 (ebook) | ISBN 9781510557352 (library binding) | ISBN 9781510557376 (ebook other)
Subjects: LCSH: A (The letter)--Juvenile literature. | English language--Vowels--Juvenile literature. | English language--Alphabet--Juvenile literature.
Classification: LCC PE1165 .R952 2022 (print) | LCC PE1165 (ebook) | DDC 421/.1--dc23
LC record available at https://lccn.loc.gov/2020054160
LC ebook record available at https://lccn.loc.gov/2020054161

Printed in Guangzhou, China
1 2 3 4 5 6 7 8 9 0 25 24 23 22 21

022021
110820

Art Director: Terry Paulhus Project Coordinator: Sara Cucini